Tarantulas

By Christy Steele

Raintree

ANIMALS OF THE RAINFOREST

www.raintreepublishers.co.uk
Visit our website to find out more information about Raintree books.

To order:
 Phone 44 (0) 1865 888112
Send a fax to 44 (0) 1865 314091
Visit the Raintree Bookshop at www.raintreepublishers.co.uk to browse our
catalogue and order online.

First published in Great Britain by
Raintree Publishers, Halley Court,
Jordan Hill, Oxford, OX2 8EJ, part of
Harcourt Education.
Raintree is a registered trademark of
Harcourt Education Ltd.

Originated by Dot Gradations Ltd
Printed and bound in Hong Kong and
China by South China

ISBN 1 844 21103 7
07 06 05 04 03
10 9 8 7 6 5 4 3 2 1

**British Library Cataloguing in
Publication Data**
Steele, Christy
Tarantulas - (Animals of the rainforest)
1. Tarantulas - Juvenile literature
2. Rainforest ecology - Juvenile
literature
I.Title
595.4'4
A catalogue for this book is available
from the British Library.

Acknowledgements
The publishers would like to thank the
following for permission to reproduce
photographs:
Corbis/Dewitt Jones, p. 26; James C.
Cokendolpher, p. **25**; Rick West, pp. 1,
4–5, 6, 10, 13, 14, 18, 20, 22, 28; ESA-
Riess, p. **16**; Warren Photographic, pp. **7,
11, 23**.

Cover photograph by Visuals Unlimited/
G and C Merker.

Every effort has been made to contact
copyright holders of any material
reproduced in this book. Any omissions
will be rectified in subsequent printings
if notice is given to the publishers.

Contents

Any words appearing in the text in bold, **like this**, are explained in the Glossary.

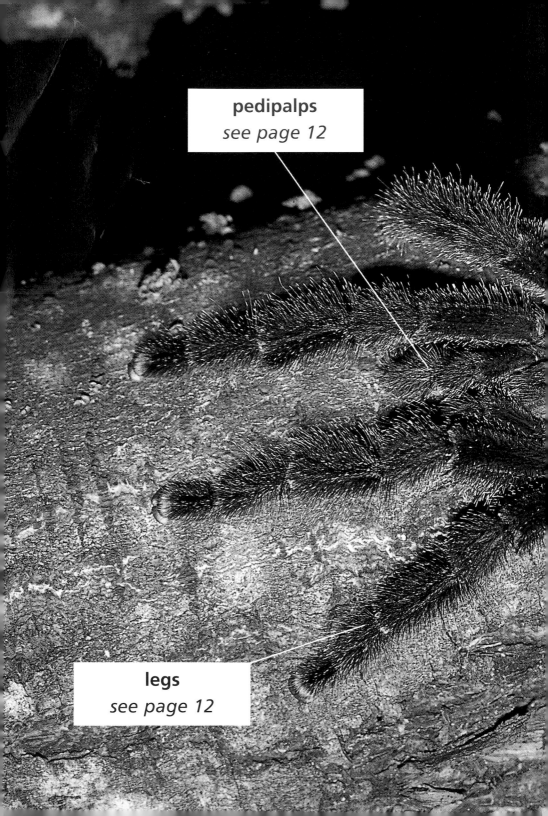

pedipalps
see page 12

legs
see page 12

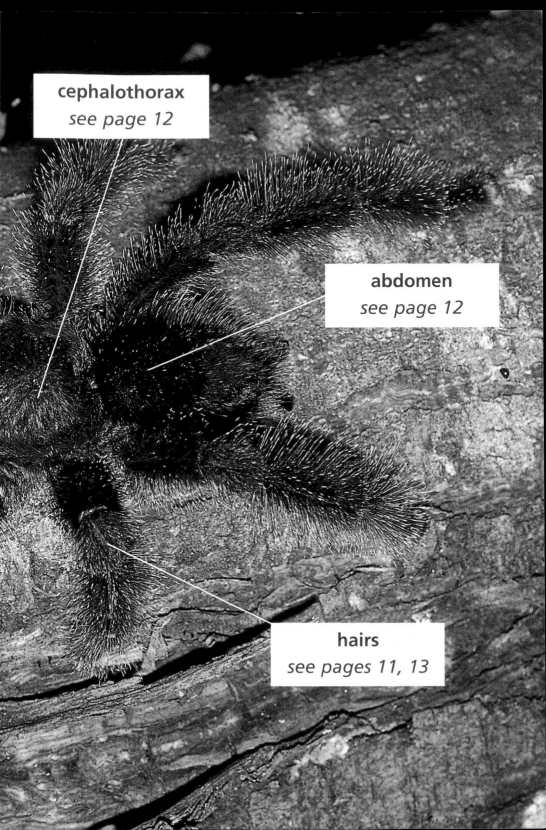

cephalothorax
see page 12

abdomen
see page 12

hairs
see pages 11, 13

USA

MEXICO

GUATEMALA
BELIZE
HONDURAS
EL SALVADOR
NICARAGUA
COSTA RICA
PANAMA

Caribbean Sea

North Atlantic
Ocean

VENEZUELA
GUYANA
SURINAM
FRENCH GUIANA

COLOMBIA

ECUADOR

Amazon River

PERU

BRAZIL

BOLIVIA

PARAGUAY

South Pacific
Ocean

URUGUAY

CHILE

ARGENTINA

South Atlantic
Ocean

N
W   E
S

Range of the tarantula in
Central and South America

Surrounding land

Sea

Borders

Rivers

A quick look at tarantulas

What do tarantulas look like?

Tarantulas are hairy spiders. Some of them are very large. They are many different colours.

How many kinds of tarantula are there?

There are about 800 known kinds of tarantula.

Where do tarantulas live?

Tarantulas live in warm places around the world. They do not live in Antarctica.

What do tarantulas eat?

Tarantulas eat meat. They catch and eat insects, frogs, lizards, mice and other small animals. They also eat spiders and other tarantulas.

Arañas peludas is the Latin American nickname for tarantulas. It means hairy spiders.

About tarantulas

Tarantulas are hairy spiders. There are about 800 known types of tarantula. Scientists think there are even more types of tarantula that have not been found yet. Some tarantulas are the largest spiders in the world.

Tarantulas live in most warm parts of the world. They do not live in Antarctica. It is too cold in Antarctica for tarantulas. Many kinds of tarantula live in rainforests. Rainforests are places where many trees and plants grow close together and rain falls most of the time. Tarantulas are important to the rainforest. They eat many insects.

This tarantula can be seen on a leaf, but its colouring helps it blend in with tree bark.

 Tarantulas have their own territories where they live and hunt. Their territories are close to their burrows or nests. A burrow is a hole where an animal lives. Tarantulas fight other tarantulas that come into their territories.

Tarantula size and colouring

Tarantulas can be many different sizes. Males are usually thinner than females.

Most tarantulas have a leg span of about 13 centimetres. Their bodies range from about 3.8 centimetres to 10 centimetres long.

Each kind of tarantula looks different. Tarantulas' hair can be black, brown, blue, red, pink, orange and many other colours. Some tarantulas have colourful markings or stripes on their bodies or legs.

A tarantula's hairs are its **sensors**. A sensor is something that can feel changes around it. Some of their hairs sense heat, cold and motion. Hairs by a tarantula's mouth help it to smell and taste.

Cephalothorax

A tarantula's body has two main parts. The front part is the **cephalothorax**. A spider's mouth, eyes and eight legs are on this part. There are two claws on each of a tarantula's legs.

Two **chelicerae** are on the sides of a tarantula's mouth. They act like a pair of jaws. A **fang** grows on the end of each of the chelicerae. A fang is a long, pointed tooth.

A tarantula has two **pedipalps** near its front legs. Pedipalps are about half the size of its legs. A tarantula uses its pedipalps to feel its way when walking. It also moves and grabs things like food with its pedipalps.

Abdomen

The back of a spider's body is its **abdomen**. Four **spinnerets** stick out from the back of the abdomen. Spiders use spinnerets to spin silk. Liquid silk is made inside tarantulas' bodies. The spinnerets shape the silk into threads. The silk hardens once it is outside the body. Tarantulas use the silk to make nests and webs to trap food.

▲ **A tarantula's fangs can grow up to about 1 centimetre long.**

Some tarantulas have special hairs on the backs of their abdomens. The hairs have very tiny hooks on them. Tarantulas can flick the hairs at their enemies. The hairs fly through the air and hurt their enemies' eyes, noses and throats.

▲ This tree-living tarantula has spun a
tube-shaped silk nest on a tree trunk.

Ground-living tarantulas

There are two groups of rainforest tarantulas.
One group stays on the ground. Most scientists
believe these tarantulas have poor eyesight.
They use their hairs to find and catch food.

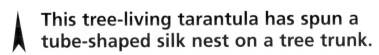

Ground-living tarantulas live in fallen logs, cracks in rocks, or **burrows**. A burrow is an underground hole or tunnel where an animal lives. Tarantulas sometimes live in burrows that other animals have left. They may also use their chelicerae to dig their own burrows. Some tarantulas spin silk to line their burrows. Others block their burrows' openings by building a mound of earth in front.

The second group of tarantulas lives mostly in trees. Tree-climbing tarantulas live in holes in trees or under branches and leaves. They may spin a tube-shaped nest of silk.

Tree-climbing tarantulas have **adapted** to live in trees. To be adapted means that a living thing has features that help it survive where it lives. These tarantulas often have longer legs and thinner abdomens than others. They have hundreds of stiff hairs on the bottoms of their feet. Their claws and hairs help them climb. They can see better than ground-living tarantulas. This helps them jump among branches. Many of them can also swim well.

This tarantula is holding an insect with its pedipalps while it eats.

Hunting and eating

Tarantulas are predators. A predator is an animal that hunts and eats other animals. Animals that are hunted are called prey. Tarantulas are also scavengers. A scavenger is an animal that eats food that it did not kill.

Tarantulas will eat almost anything they can catch. Insects are a common food. They often eat ants, beetles and cockroaches. They may also eat small lizards, snakes and frogs. They will even eat other tarantulas.

Tarantulas are **nocturnal**. Nocturnal means active during the night. They rest in their burrows during the day. At night, they come out to hunt. They never go far from their burrows when they hunt.

Tree frogs and lizards are common foods for tree-living tarantulas.

Finding and catching prey

Both ground-living and tree-living tarantulas find prey in the same way. A tarantula's hairs sense when prey comes near. They also use silk threads strung around their burrows or nests. The threads move when prey comes close.

Tarantulas hunt by sitting still and waiting. Some tarantulas hide in their nests or burrows. Others have colours that blend with their surroundings. This makes it hard for prey to see them. They may sit on tree branches or under leaves. Tarantulas wait until prey comes close. Then they race out and jump on prey. Tarantulas use their legs and pedipalps to hold prey still.

Tarantulas sink their sharp fangs into the prey's body. A tarantula fang is hollow with a hole in the end. When a tarantula bites, **venom** fills its fangs. Venom is a kind of poison. The tarantula pushes the venom into its prey's body. The venom makes the prey unable to move.

Tarantulas' mouths are so small that only liquid can fit through them. To eat, they put special digestive juices on to their prey. Digestive juices break down the prey's bodies into liquid. They cut up the prey with their chelicerae and pedipalps to help make it liquid. The tarantula then drinks the liquid prey.

Only tarantulas of the same species can mate with each other.

A tarantula's life cycle

Tarantulas live and hunt by themselves. They come together only to mate.

Tarantulas cannot mate until they are fully grown. Each type of tarantula takes a different length of time to become fully grown. Some types are fully grown at two years, but others take ten years or more to grow.

Male tarantulas will travel a long way to look for females. A male is careful when he finds a female. He uses his legs to tap the female's burrow. When she comes out, he taps her as well. He also may shake his legs. The tapping and shaking show her that he is not an enemy. After mating, the male leaves. Otherwise, the female may try to eat him.

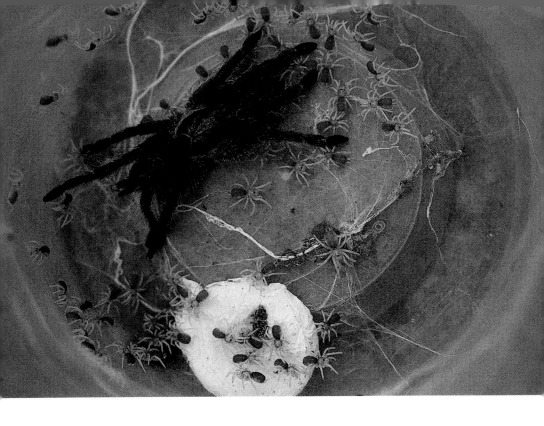

Spiderlings grow inside the egg sac.
Large spiderlings eat smaller ones.

Laying eggs

Females lay eggs several weeks or months
after mating. They spin a pad of silk. They lay
hundreds of eggs on the silk pad. Then they
cover the eggs with more silk and seal the silk
covering. This makes one large egg sac. The
silk covers the eggs and keeps them safe.

 Tarantula hawk wasps are enemies of tarantulas. If they meet, a tarantula hawk wasp and a tarantula will fight to the death. If the wasp wins, it stings the spider many times, which makes it unable to move. Then the wasp lays an egg on the tarantula. When the egg hatches, the young wasp feeds on the living tarantula.

The females never leave their egg sacs. They carry their egg sacs wherever they go.

Young tarantulas grow inside the eggs for one to three months. Then they hatch. After hatching, they are called **spiderlings**. Spiderlings grow inside the egg sac for a while. Then they break out of the egg sac. Spiderlings may stay near their mother for a short time. Then they walk away to find their own burrow.

Only a few spiderlings live to become adults. Tarantulas have many enemies. Frogs, lizards, birds, insects and other spiders eat many spiderlings. Owls, millipedes, snakes and other animals eat adult tarantulas.

Moulting

A hard, outer skin covers tarantulas. After time, new skin grows underneath the old skin. The tarantula must shed the old skin. This is called **moulting**. Tarantulas stop eating a few days before they moult. Some tarantulas spin a silk pad to rest on during their moult.

To moult, the tarantula flips on its back or side. It moves itself back and forth until it is free of its old skin. A moult may last from two hours to two days. Tarantulas are weak during this time. Tarantulas' new skin is soft. It takes several days for it to become hard.

Tarantulas can grow back missing legs, spinnerets or fangs when they moult. Sometimes tarantulas flick off all the hairs from their abdomens. This leaves a bald spot. Those hairs grow back when the spider moults.

Young tarantulas moult from two to ten times a year. Older, full-grown female tarantulas moult once a year or less. Males do not moult once they are adults.

This moulting tarantula is pulling its legs out of its old skin.

The length of a tarantula's life depends on what kind it is. But all females live longer than males. Some female tarantulas can live for 30 years or more. Males often die within a few days or a few months after they start mating. Some tree-living males may live for up to two years after mating.

People must be careful when they handle their pet tarantulas.

Tarantulas and people

People and tarantulas have been living together for thousands of years. In the rainforest, people eat tarantulas. They wrap them in leaves and cook them. The tarantulas are important sources of food for these people.

Some people around the world keep tarantulas as pets. Tarantulas need only small spaces to live. People feed them mice, raw meat or live insects, such as beetles or crickets.

Ground-living tarantulas can be easily hurt. Their abdomens could split if they are dropped. This could kill them. You must be careful when touching or picking up tarantulas.

Tarantulas give warnings before they bite.
They raise their two front legs.

Tarantula bites

Many people fear tarantulas. They believe that
tarantulas will try to hunt and bite them. But
this is not true. Tarantulas try to stay away from
people. They often hide.

Tarantulas may bite if people scare them or
try to pick them up. Some people say the bites

feel like bee stings. The bites may become red and itch. But there are no known cases of people dying from tarantula bites.

Future of tarantulas

People are cutting down the rainforest to build houses and clear land for farming. Many tarantulas lose their homes when this happens. Many kinds of tarantulas die when the rainforest is cut down. Some tarantulas can live near people. They may make their burrows on buildings, in old boxes or in holes in walls.

Selling tarantulas as pets may affect the number of tarantulas in the wild. The Mexican redknee is one kind of common pet tarantula. So many are caught and sold that they are in danger of dying out in the wild.

The number of wild tarantulas is falling in many places around the world. People can keep them safe by working to save the rainforests where tarantulas live.

Glossary

abdomen back part of a spider's body

adapt to change to survive well in a place

burrow underground hole or tunnel where an
  animal lives

cephalothorax front part of a spider's body

chelicerae two body parts around spiders'
  mouths that are used like jaws

fang long, pointed tooth

moult to shed the old outer skin in order to
  grow

nocturnal active at night

pedipalps pair of body parts on spider's
  cephalothorax, which it uses to feel its way
  and grab prey

sensor animal's body part that can feel changes
  around it

spiderling young spider

spinneret a body part through which spiders
  produce silk

venom poison made by some animals and
  insects that is pushed into their prey or
  enemies

More information

Internet sites

Enchanted Learning
www.EnchantedLearning.com

Really Wild Zone
www.bbc.co.uk/reallywild/amazing

Useful address

World Wildlife Fund-UK
Panda House, Weyside Park
Godalming, Surrey, GU7 1XR

Books to read

Hartley, K; Macro, C. *Bug Books: Spider.*
Heinemann Library, Oxford, 2000
Theodorou, R; Telford, C. *Amazing Journeys:*
Up a Rainforest Tree, Heinemann Library,
Oxford, 1998

Index